RICE RICE

The Saga Continues

50 Unique Rice Cooker Recipes

I Chose To Stop Somewhere In Between Here. Care To Join Me?

Dexter Poin

AKA Chef Boy R Dex

AKA The Rice Cooker Ripper

AKA The Little Self Publisher That Did, & Does
AKA Whatever You Feel Like Calling Me
Recipe Junkies

Hey, how is life? I hope that all is well, & I am not just saying that, in order to get on your good side.

I genuinely do wish well on everyone, even people I cannot stand, because I believe in a little thing called karma, or what goes around, comes around, or whatever other little saying that is out there, that basically means we reap what we sow.

If you have no clue who I am, well, this little recipe book will not be much help on providing you with that info, as it is just a bunch of recipes. Hopefully, you find at least some of them, to be delicious?

If you are someone who may be interested in other things that I do, and what I am all about, then simply just go to my website at paradigmpublishingconsulting.com

There, you will find all kinds of links directing you to things I do online. All of my Amazon page links are there as well. If you are interested in the Recipe Junkies FREE newsletter, then go to   Facebook   here: **https://www.facebook.com/recipejunkies/** & links are pinned to the top of that page.

Enjoy, & Carpe Diem

Dexter

Rice Cooker Oats

Red Beans and Rice

Toasted Coconut Yellow Rice

Southwest Quinoa

Vegan Lentil Bolognese

Vegan Lentil Chili

Smoky Cajun Black Eyed Peas

Pasta and Veggies

Rice Cooker Barley

Rice Cooker Risotto

Sweet Potato Curry

Spinach Rice

Rice Cooker Chana Masala

Vegan Butter Chickpeas

Vegan Gumbo

Rice Cooker Muffin Cake

Rice Pudding

Poached Pomegranate Spiced Pears

Rice Cooker Chocolate Cake

Almond Vanilla Steel cut Oatmeal

Vegan Cajun Wild Rice

Rice Cooker Vegan Pasta Cubano

Vegan Jambalaya

Quinoa and Black beans

Rice Cooker Polenta

Vegan Taco Soup

Vegan Red Lentil Soup

Winter Lentil Vegetable Soup

Rice Cooker Cauliflower Rice

Curried Quinoa

Spicy Beans, Rice and Corn

Chickpea, Red Lentil and Pumpkin Curry

Vegetarian Minestrone

Rice Cooker Applesauce

Coconut Tapioca Pudding

Rice Cooker Rice Pilaf

Rice Cooker Mexican Rice

Rice Cooker Fried Rice

Lemon Rice

Caribbean Rice

Rice Cooker Spanish Rice

Rice and Black Beans

Rice Cooker Vegan Pancake

Carrot Rice with Peanuts

Vegan White and Black Bean Soup

Rice Cooker Vegan Frittata

Pomegranate and Quinoa Salad

Rice Cooker Cabbage Stir Fry

Rice Cooker Smoky Orange Rice

Rice Cooker Jamaican Grits

Rice Cooker Oats

Serves: 2

Preparation Time: 20 minutes

Ingredients

- Oats (1 cup, quick cook)
- Soy Milk (1 cup)
- Vanilla (1 teaspoon)
- Water (1 cup)
- Honey (2 tablespoons)
- Salt
- White sugar (1 tablespoon)

Directions

1. Put all ingredients in rice cooker and stir to combine.
2. Cook for 15-20 minutes.
3. Serve!

Nutritional Information

Calories 300

Carbs 50g

Protein 7.4g

Fat 4g

Red Beans and Rice

Serves: 4-6

Preparation Time: 40 minutes

Ingredients

- Red beans (30 oz. can, rinsed and drained)
- Green pepper (1 cup, diced)
- Thyme (2 teaspoons, dried)
- Vegetable broth (2 1/3 cups)
- Paprika (1 teaspoon, smoked)
- Rice (1 cup)
- Onion (1 cup, diced)
- Celery (1 cup, chopped)
- Garlic (3 cloves, diced)
- Bay leaf (1)
- Cayenne pepper (1/4 teaspoon)

Directions

1. Add red beans, green pepper, thyme, broth, paprika, onion, celery, garlic, cayenne pepper and bay leaf to cooker.
2. Stir to combine and cook for 10 minutes or until thoroughly heated then add rice and stir.
3. Cover rice cooker and cook for 30 minutes or until all liquid has dissolved.
4. Fluff rice using a fork and serve!

Nutritional Information

Calories 660

Carbs 122g

Protein 41g

Fat 2g

Toasted Coconut Yellow Rice

Serves: 8

Preparation Time: 45 minutes

Ingredients

- White rice (2 cups, washed)
- Water (1 ¼ cups)
- Ground turmeric (1 teaspoon)
- Coconut milk (14 oz., unsweetened)
- Coconut flakes (1/4 cup, unsweetened)
- Kosher salt (1/2 teaspoon)
- Green onions (1/2 cup)
- Thyme (1 teaspoon, dried)

Directions

1. Add coconut milk, thyme, green onions, turmeric, salt and half of coconut flakes to a saucepan and cook for 5 minutes until turmeric dissolves.
2. Add rice to cooker and then cover with coconut milk blend.
3. Set cooker and allow rice to cook for 20-25 minutes. Let rice stay in cooker on warm setting for 5 minutes.
4. Toast remaining coconut flakes in a skillet until golden.
5. Fluff rice using a fork and serve topped with toasted flakes.

Nutritional Information

Calories 277

Carbs 39.7g

Protein 4.4g

Fat 11.4g

Southwest Quinoa

Serves: 10

Preparation Time: 1 hour 10 minutes

Ingredients

- Black beans (30 oz. can, rinsed)
- Quinoa (12 oz.)
- Taco seasoning (1.25 oz.)
- Tomatoes (20 oz. can, diced)
- Green chile pepper (1/2 cup, diced)
- Vegetable broth (2 cups)

Directions

1. Combine all ingredients in rice cooker.
2. Set cooker on 'brown rice' mode and cook for 60 minutes.
3. Fluff rice with a fork and serve!

Nutritional Information

Calories 221

Carbs 40.1g

Protein 10.3g

Fat 2.3g

Vegan Lentil Bolognese

Serves: 7

Preparation Time: 3 hours 15 minutes

Ingredients

- Plum tomatoes (28 oz., whole peeled, salt free)
- Pepper (1 cup, chopped)
- Onions (1 cup, chopped)
- Pomi tomatoes (26 oz., strained)
- Maple syrup (2 tablespoons)
- Basil (1 tablespoon. dried)
- Sea salt (2 teaspoons)
- Black pepper (1/4 teaspoon)
- Brown lentils (1 cups, rinsed)
- Vegetable broth (4 cups, low salt)
- Garlic (6 cloves, crushed)
- Oregano (1 tablespoon, dried)
- Parsley (1/2 tablespoon, dried)

Directions

1. Add plum tomatoes to cooker and use spoon to break up.
2. Put in remaining ingredients and stir to combine.
3. Set cooker to 'white rice' mode and cook until cycle ends. Stir and repeat cycle 2 more times. Test if lentils are cooked and repeat cycle if necessary.
4. Keep on warm until ready to serve.

Nutritional Information

Calories 250

Carbs 53g **Protein** 13g

Fat 1.5 g

Vegan Lentil Chili

Serves: 8

Preparation Time: 1 hour 15 minutes

Ingredients

- Red Lentils (1 cup, rinsed)
- Red onions (1 ½ cups, diced)
- Garlic (2 cloves, diced)
- Chili powder (2 tablespoons)
- Cannellini beans (15 oz., rinsed and drained)
- Tamari soy sauce (2 tablespoons)
- Tomatoes (2 cups, diced)
- Celery (1/2 cup, diced)
- Cumin (1 tablespoon)
- Black beans (15 oz., rinsed and drained)
- Vegetable broth (6 cups)
- Brown rice (8 cups)

Directions

1. Add all ingredients to rice cooker and stir to combine.
2. Set on 'brown rice' mode and cook until rice has softened. Add more liquid if necessary.
3. Cook until chili has thickened. Keep warm until ready to serve.

Nutritional Information

Calories 570

Carbs 111g

Protein 27g

Fat 4 g

Smoky Cajun Black Eyed Peas

Serves: 8

Preparation Time: 2 hours 15 minutes

Ingredients

- White onion (1/2, chopped)
- Bell pepper (1, green, diced)
- Celery (2,ribs, chopped)
- Tomatoes (28 oz., can, crushed)
- Oregano (2 teaspoons, dried)
- Liquid smoke (2 teaspoons)
- Black pepper (1/4 teaspoon)
- Leafy greens (1 cup, chopped) - spinach, kale etc.
- Garlic (2 cloves, diced)
- Bell pepper (1, red, diced)
- Vegetable broth/water (1/2 cup)
- Paprika (1 ½ tablespoons, smoked)
- Thyme (1 teaspoon, dried)
- Salt (1 teaspoon)
- Cayenne pepper (1 teaspoon)
- Black-eyed peas (2 ½ cups, cooked)
- Pasta (1 lb., preferably spaghetti)

Directions

1. Add all ingredients to rice cooker except pasta and stir to combine.
2. Cook for 30 minutes or until sauce has thickened; keep warm while you prepare pasta.
3. Prepare pasta as directed on package, drain and serve with peas.

Nutritional Information

Calories 470 **Carbs** 88g **Protein** 22g **Fat** 4 g

Pasta and Veggies

Serves: 6

Preparation Time: 45 minutes

Ingredients

- Pasta sauce (48 oz.)
- Mixed vegetables (20 oz., frozen)
- Water (3 cups)
- Pasta (16 oz., gluten-free)
- Spinach (1 cup)
- Parmesan cheese (vegan)

Directions

1. Thaw vegetables and then add to cooker along with water, pasta and pasta sauce. Stir to combine.
2. Set cooker on 'white rice' mode and cook for 20 minutes. Stir pasta halfway and continue cooking for an additional 20 minutes.
3. Serve topped with vegan cheese.

Nutritional Information

Calories 480

Carbs 89g

Protein 15g

Fat 8g

Rice Cooker Barley

Serves: 5

Preparation Time: 1 hour 10 minutes

Ingredients

- Vegetable broth (2 cups)
- Barley (1/2 cup, hulled)
- Mixed peppers (1/2 cup, chopped)
- Chili powder (1 teaspoon)
- Canned tomatoes (15 oz., diced)
- Onion (1/2, chopped)
- Paprika (1 teaspoon)
- Cumin (1 teaspoon)

Directions

1. Add all ingredients to rice cooker and stir to combine.
2. Set on 'brown rice' mode and cook for 30 minutes. Stir and cook for an additional 30 minutes.
3. Keep warm until ready to serve.

Nutritional Information

Calories 105

Carbs 20.3g

Protein 4g

Fat 0.9 g

Rice Cooker Risotto

Serves: 6

Preparation Time: 45 minutes

Ingredients

- Arborio rice (2 ½ cups)
- Parmesan cheese (1 cup, vegan)
- Vegetable broth (4 ½ cups)
- Shiitake mushrooms (3 oz., sliced)
- Butternut squash (4 cups, cubed)
- White wine (1 cup, dry)
- Salt
- Black pepper
- Parsley (1/2 cup, chopped)

Directions

1. Add all ingredients to rice cooker except cheese and stir to combine.
2. Set on 'brown rice' mode and cook until rice has softened for about 40 minutes.
3. Keep warm until ready to serve.
4. Add cheese, stir and serve.

Nutritional Information

Calories 328

Carbs 56.9g

Protein 9.4g

Fat 4.3 g

Sweet Potato Curry

Serves: 4

Preparation Time: 40 minutes

Ingredients

- Curry paste (3 tablespoons)
- Sweet potatoes (2, large, peeled and cubed)
- Chickpeas (15 oz.)
- Coconut milk (16 oz.)
- Onion (1, chopped)
- Red pepper (1, diced)
- Spinach (6 cups)
- Olive oil

Directions

1. Heat rice cooker and add oil, put in onion and sauté for 3minutes then add curry and stir; cook for 1 minute.
2. Add all remaining ingredients except spinach and stir to combine.
3. Cook for 30 minutes then add spinach and stir.
4. Cook for an additional 10 minutes until spinach wilts.
5. Serve.

Nutritional Information

Calories 319

Carbs 82g

Protein 21g

Fat 4 g

Spinach Rice

Serves: 4

Preparation Time: 2 hours 15 minutes

Ingredients

- Vegetable oil (1 tablespoon)
- Onion (1, diced)
- Green chili peppers (4, chopped)
- Fresh spinach (1 ½ cups)
- Coriander powder (1 teaspoon, roasted)
- Water (4 ½ cups)
- Cumin seeds (1 teaspoon)
- Carrot (1, diced)
- Garlic-ginger paste (1 teaspoon)
- White rice (2 cups, uncooked)
- Salt

Directions

1. Heat skillet then add oil and heat thoroughly then add cumin and cook for a minute until fragrant.
2. Add carrot, chile peppers and onion, stir and cook for 5 minutes till veggies are tender. Add garlic paste and cook for 5 more minutes.
3. Put spinach in a processor and pulse until pasty then add to skillet and stir. Cook for 2-3 minutes until water evaporates. Add rice to mixture and stir to combine.
4. Transfer to rice cooker and cover with water.
5. Cook for 20 minutes.
6. Fluff with a fork and serve.

Nutritional Information

Calories 410 **Carbs** 82.5g **Protein** 8.3g

Fat 4.4 g

Rice Cooker Chana Masala

Serves: 9

Preparation Time: 2 hours 10 minutes

Ingredients

- Chickpeas (29 oz., drained)
- Tomatoes (2, large)
- Potatoes (2, large, diced)
- Ginger (1" piece, chopped)
- Cumin seed (1/2 teaspoon, powdered)
- Masala (1 tablespoon)
- Chaat masala (1 teaspoon)
- Cayenne (1 teaspoon)
- Salt
- Onion (1, chopped)
- Tomato paste (2 tablespoons)
- Garlic (4 cloves)
- Bay leaves (2)
- Coriander seeds (1 tablespoon)
- Turmeric (1/4 teaspoon)
- Paprika (1 teaspoon)
- Water

Directions

1. Put tomatoes, ginger, onion and garlic in a processor or blender and puree.
2. Pour mixture into rice cooker along with all remaining ingredients; add 3cupsof water to mixture and stir.
3. Set cooker on 'brown rice' mode and cook for 40 minutes, add more water and repeat cooking cycle twice.
4. Let chana masala keep warm until ready to serve.

Nutritional Information Calories 420 **Carbs** 74g **Protein** 20g **Fat** 6g

---

Vegan Butter Chickpeas

Serves: 5

Preparation Time: 1 hour 15 minutes

Ingredients

- Coconut oil (1 tablespoon)
- Garlic (3 cloves, diced)
- Coconut milk (14 oz.)
- Curry powder (1 tablespoon)
- Tofu (1 lb., pressed and cubed)
- Onion (1, chopped)
- Ginger (1 tablespoon, chopped)
- Tomato paste (6 oz.)
- Chickpeas (3 cups, cooked)

Directions

1. Heat rice cooker and add oil then sauté onion for 3 minutes. Add ginger and garlic and cook for an additional 3 minutes.
2. Add coconut milk and stir to combine. Put in all remaining ingredients and cook for 60 minutes. Check if mixture has thickened, if not cook for additional time until desired consistency is achieved.
3. Keep warm until ready to serve.

Nutritional Information

Calories 460

Carbs 90g

Protein 34g

Fat 34 g

Vegan Gumbo

Serves: 8

Preparation Time: 1 hour 30 minutes

Ingredients

- Vegetable oil (3 tablespoons)
- Tomato (1, chopped)
- Garlic (6 cloves, diced)
- Creole mustard (2 tablespoons)
- Apple cider vinegar (1 tablespoon)
- Soy sauce (1 teaspoon)
- Red pepper flakes (1 teaspoon)
- Nutmeg (1/4 teaspoon)
- Vegetable broth (4 cups)
- Red beans (16 oz., drained)
- Zucchini (1 ½ cups, chopped)
- Red bell pepper (1 ½ cups, minced)
- Flour (3 tablespoons)
- Onion (1 ½ cups, chopped)
- Worcestershire sauce (1 tablespoon, vegan)
- Liquid smoke (1 ½ teaspoons)
- Hot sauce (1/2 teaspoon)
- Thyme (1 teaspoon, dried)
- Paprika (1 tablespoon, smoked)
- Oregano (1 teaspoon, dried)
- Okra (4 cups, sliced)
- Cremini mushrooms (8, cut into quarters)
- Green bell pepper (1 ½ cups, diced)
- Celery (1 cup, sliced thin)
- Green onion (1/2 cup)

Directions

1. Heat oil over a medium flame in a Dutch oven and add flour. Whisk mixture for 5 minutes until fragrant. Lower heat and cook for 25 minutes, whisking often to avoid burning. Cook until mixture is golden and remove from heat.
2. Put tomato, garlic, mustard, vinegar, soy sauce, red pepper flakes, nutmeg, oregano, onion, Worcestershire sauce, liquid smoke, hot sauce, thyme and paprika into a food processor. Pulse until mixture is thoroughly combined.
3. Add mixture to flour in Dutch oven and whisk to combine. Transfer to rice cooker and add remaining ingredients except green onions. Stir to combine and cook for 40 minutes. Check consistency and repeat cycle until desired consistency is achieved.
4. Keep warm until ready to serve.
5. Serve with rice and top with green onions.

Nutritional Information

Calories 600

Carbs 96g

Protein 23g

Fat 7 g

Rice Cooker Muffin Cake

Serves: 8

Preparation Time: 2 hours 15 minutes

Ingredients

- Flour (1 cup)
- Baking powder (2 ½ teaspoons)
- Salt (1/4 teaspoon)
- Coconut milk (1 cup)
- Nutmeg (1 ½ teaspoons, ground)
- Apple (1/2 cup, minced)
- Raisins (1/3 cup)
- White sugar (1/3 cup, vegan friendly)
- Baking soda (1 teaspoon)
- Bran flakes (1 ½ cups, crushed)
- Cinnamon (1 ½ teaspoons)
- Vanilla (1 ½ teaspoons)
- Olive oil (1/4 cup)
- Banana (1/2 cup, diced)
- Cooking spray

Directions

1. Use cooking spray to coat rice cooker.
2. Combine flour, baking powder, salt, sugar and baking soda together in a bowl. In another bowl combine milk, nutmeg, vanilla, bran flakes and cinnamon; put aside to soak for 5 minutes.
3. Add oil to soaked bran flakes and stir then add flour mixture to wet mix. Mix together until thoroughly combined, add banana, raisins and apple and fold gently.
4. Add mixture to rice cooker and cook for 40 minutes or until cake is done.
5. Serve warm or cool.

Nutritional Information Calories 230 **Carbs** 37g **Protein** 4.4g **Fat** 6 g

Rice Pudding

Serves: 4

Preparation Time: 45 minutes

Ingredients

- Rice (1 cup)
- Sugar (1/2 cup, vegan friendly)
- Soy milk (2 ¾ cups)
- Vanilla (1 teaspoon)
- Cinnamon (1/4 teaspoon)
- Soy milk (1 cup)

Directions

1. Put 2 ¾ cups milk and rice into rice cooker, stir and set to cook for 15 minutes.
2. Open cooker and add vanilla, cinnamon and sugar. Stir to combine and cook for an additional 15 minutes or until desired consistency is achieved. Add leftover milk and turn off cooker.
3. Serve warm or cool. Can be topped with dried fruit.

Nutritional Information

Calories 310

Carbs 66g

Protein 10.6g

Fat 0.4 g

Poached Pomegranate Spiced Pears

Serves: 4

Preparation Time: 55 minutes

Ingredients

- Pears (2 Bosc/Anjou, firm, peel and core removed and halved)
- Apple cider (2 cups)
- Clementine peel
- Star anise (2)
- Ginger (1" piece, sliced)
- Pomegranate juice (2 cups)
- Cinnamon stick (1)
- Cloves (2, whole)
- Cardamom pods (3, black)

Directions

1. Add apple cider, clementine peel, anise, ginger, pomegranate juice, cinnamon stick, cloves and cardamom to rice cooker. Stir to combine and add pears to liquid.
2. Cook for 50 minutes or until pears are tender.
3. Turn off cooker and flip over pears; let them sit in liquid for 60 minutes. Repeat once more.
4. Serve as is or chill in liquid until ready to serve.

Nutritional Information

Calories 462

Carbs 98g

Protein 1g

Fat 0.4 g

Rice Cooker Chocolate Cake

Serves: 8

Preparation Time: 1 hour

Ingredients

- Flour (1 ½ cups)
- Cocoa powder (1/4 cup)
- Salt (1/2 teaspoon)
- Vanilla (1 teaspoon)
- Water (1 cup)
- White sugar (1 cup, vegan friendly)
- Baking soda (1 teaspoon)
- Vegetable oil (1/3 cup)
- White vinegar (1 teaspoon, distilled)
- Baking powder (1/4 teaspoon)
- Cooking spray

Directions

1. Use cooking spray to coat rice cooker.
2. Combine flour, cocoa powder, baking powder, salt, sugar and baking soda together in a bowl.
3. Add wet ingredients to dry mixture and mix until thoroughly combined. Be careful not to overmix.
4. Add mixture to rice cooker and cook for 45 minutes or until cake is done.
5. Keep cake warm for 15 minutes then remove bowl from cooker and put aside to cool.
6. Invert onto a plate and serve.

Nutritional Information

Calories 154.6 **Carbs** 21.4g **Protein** 2g

Fat 6.9 g

Almond Vanilla Steel cut Oatmeal

Serves: 2-4

Preparation Time: 40 minutes

Ingredients

- Steel cut oats (1 cup)
- Water (1 ½ cups)
- Salt (1/2 teaspoon)
- Brown sugar
- Soy milk (2 cups, unsweetened)
- Vanilla (2 teaspoons)
- Almonds (raw, sliced)
- Maple syrup

Directions

1. Add milk, vanilla, salt, oatmeal and water to rice cooker.
2. Cook oats on porridge setting or for 40 minutes until thoroughly cooked.
3. Sweetened with sugar and/or maple syrup.
4. Serve topped with almonds

Nutritional Information

Calories 288

Carbs 38g

Protein 8.4g

Fat 8 g

Vegan Cajun Wild Rice

Serves: 6

Preparation Time: 1 hour 5 minutes

Ingredients

- Wild rice (1 cup, uncooked)
- Water (1/4 cup)
- Sweet onion (1/2 cup, diced)
- Garlic (1 tablespoon, diced)
- Vegetable broth (14 oz.)
- Vegan Sausage (1/2 lb., sliced)
- Mushrooms (1 cup, fresh, chopped)
- Coconut cream (1 ½ cups)
- Creole seasoning (1 teaspoon)
- Cayenne pepper (1/2 teaspoon)
- Bell peppers (1 cup, chopped)

Directions

1. Add all ingredients except coconut cream to rice cooker.
2. Cook for 50 minutes and check rice if cooked.
3. Add coconut cream to rice and use fork to fluff and combine.
4. Keep warm for 15 minutes.
5. Serve.

Nutritional Information

Calories 248

Carbs 21g

Protein 9g

Fat 12 g

Rice Cooker Vegan Pasta Cubano

Serves: 3

Preparation Time: 40 minutes

Ingredients

- Olive oil (1 tablespoon)
- Bell peppers (1 cup, diced)
- Salt
- Oregano (1 teaspoon, dried)
- Water (2 cups)
- Green olives (2 tablespoons, sliced)
- Macaroni (2 cups, elbow, uncooked)
- Veggie mincemeat (200 grams)
- Onion (1/2 cup, diced)
- Cumin (1 teaspoon)
- Worcestershire sauce (2 tablespoons, vegan)
- Tomatoes (1 cup, diced)
- Olive oil (1 teaspoon)
- Parmesan cheese (vegan)

Directions

1. Soak veggie mince as directed on package and drain.
2. Heat 1 tablespoon oil in a pan then add onions and bell peppers; sauté for 3 minutes until tender.
3. Add veggie mince to pot along with oregano, cumin and add salt to taste. Stir to combine and cook until mince is browned. Add Worcestershire sauce and stir to combine.
4. Transfer mince to rice cooker along with water, olives, pasta, tomatoes and leftover olive oil.
5. Cook for 25 minutes or until pasta is cooked. Add more water if necessary. Try not to overcook pasta and do not keep on warm as pasta will be soggy.
6. Serve topped with cheese.

Nutritional Information

Calories 412

Carbs 40g

Protein 4g

Fat 10 g

Vegan Jambalaya

Serves: 6-8

Preparation Time: 60 minutes

Ingredients

- Vegan sausage (1/2 lb., smoked, sliced)
- Water (3/4 cup)
- Black-eyed peas (1 can, with liquid)
- French onion soup (1/2 cup)
- Tomatoes (1 can, diced with liquid)
- Rice (2 cups, uncooked)
- Cajun seasoning (1/2 teaspoon)
- Bell peppers (1/2 cup)

Directions

1. Add all ingredients to rice cooker and stir to combine.
2. Set cooker and cook for 30 minutes or until rice is cooked.
3. Keep warm for 5 minutes and then check rice. Add more water and cook for an additional 15 minutes if necessary.
4. Serve.

Nutritional Information

Calories 345

Carbs 35g

Protein 9.4g

Fat 8.4 g

Quinoa and Black beans

Serves: 10

Preparation Time: 40 minutes

Ingredients

- Vegetable oil (1 teaspoon)
- Garlic (3 cloves, chopped)
- Vegetable broth (1 ½ cups)
- Cayenne pepper (1/4 teaspoon)
- Corn kernels (1 cup, frozen)
- Fresh cilantro (1/2 cup, chopped)
- Onion (1, chopped)
- Quinoa (3/4 cup)
- Cumin (1 teaspoon)
- Salt
- Black pepper
- Black beans (15 oz., can, rinsed)

Directions

1. Heat oil in rice cooker and sauté garlic and onions for 5 minutes.
2. Add quinoa to cooker along with broth, cumin, salt, black pepper and cayenne pepper.
3. Cook for 20 minutes then add remaining ingredients. Stir to combine and cook for an additional 10-15 minutes.
4. Serve.

Nutritional Information

Calories 153

Carbs 27.8g

Protein 7.7g

Fat 1.7 g

Rice Cooker Polenta

Serves: 4

Preparation Time: 40 minutes

Ingredients

- Butter (2 tablespoons, preferably vegan friendly)
- Garlic (1 glove, diced)
- Coconut milk (1 cup)
- Salt (1/4 teaspoon)
- Parmesan cheese (2 oz., vegan, shredded)
- Onion (1/2, chopped)
- Vegetable broth (1 cup)
- Polenta (1/2 cup)
- Vegan cheddar (2 oz.)
- Black pepper (1/4 teaspoon)

Directions

1. Put butter, garlic and onion in rice cooker. Turn on cooker and close lid; cook for 10 minutes until onion is tender.
2. Add milk, salt and broth then add polenta and stir.
3. Cook for 30-40 minutes until liquid is absorbed. Be sure to stir polenta occasionally.
4. Turn off cooker and add cheeses and pepper. Stir until combined.
5. Serve.

Nutritional Information

Calories 297

Carbs 20.8g

Protein 14.2g

Fat 17.5 g

Vegan Taco Soup

Serves: 3-4

Preparation Time: 1 hour 10 minutes

Ingredients

- Onion (1/2, chopped)
- Olive oil (1 tablespoon)
- Vegetable broth (5 cups, low salt)
- Tomatoes (1 can, diced)
- Corn kernels (1 cup, frozen)
- Garlic (1 clove, chopped)
- Tofu (2 cups, firm, cubed)
- Carrot (1 cup, chopped)
- Brown rice (1/2 cup, uncooked)
- Black beans (1/2 cup, canned)
- Taco seasoning (1 pack)

Directions

1. Heat oil in a rice cooker and sauté garlic and onion until slightly golden.
2. Add cubed tofu to cooker and cook for 5-10 minutes until golden.
3. Add all remaining ingredients to cooker and cook for 45-60 minutes.
4. Serve.

Nutritional Information

Calories 295

Carbs 32g

Protein 14.5g

Fat 11g

Vegan Red Lentil Soup

Serves: 4

Preparation Time: 55 minutes

Ingredients

- Peanut oil (1 tablespoon)
- Ginger (1 tablespoon, diced)
- Fenugreek seeds
- Butternut squash (1 cup, peel, seeds removed and cubed)
- Vegetable broth (2 cups, low salt)
- Tomato paste (2 tablespoons)
- Cayenne pepper
- Salt
- Onion (1, chopped)
- Garlic (1 clove, chopped)
- Red lentils (1 cup, dry)
- Cilantro (1/3 cup, chopped)
- Coconut milk (7 oz.)
- Curry powder (1 teaspoon)
- Nutmeg
- Black pepper

Directions

1. Heat oil in rice cooker and sauté fenugreek, garlic, ginger and onion until onion is soft.
2. Add remaining ingredients to cooker and stir to combine.
3. Cook for 40 minutes or until squash and lentils are tender.
4. Keep warm for 10 minutes after done cooking.
5. Serve.

Nutritional Information

Calories 303

Carbs 34.2g

Protein 13g

Fat 14.6 g

Winter Lentil Vegetable Soup

Serves: 6

Preparation Time: 40 minutes

Ingredients

- Green lentils (1/2 cup)
- Celery (1 stalk, chopped)
- Tomatoes (28 oz. can, whole, chopped)
- Carrots (3, chopped)
- Salt (1 teaspoon)
- White sugar (1/4 teaspoon, vegan friendly)
- Thyme (1/2 teaspoon, dried)
- Onion (1 cup, chopped)
- Cabbage (2 cups, shredded)
- Vegetable broth (2 cups)
- Garlic (1 clove, crushed)
- Black pepper (1/2 teaspoon)
- Basil (1/2 teaspoon, dried)
- Curry powder (1/4 teaspoon)

Directions

1. Add all ingredients to rice cooker except cabbage.
2. Cook for 30 minutes, stir and add cabbage to mixture; cook for an additional 10 minutes. Add water if mixture is too thick.
3. Serve.

Nutritional Information

Calories 107

Carbs 21.6g

Protein 6g

Fat 0.5g

Rice Cooker Cauliflower Rice

Serves: 10

Preparation Time: 15 minutes

Ingredients

- Cauliflower (1 head, large)
- Water (1 cup)
- Green onions (1bunch, diced)
- Salt (1 teaspoon)
- Potatoes (3, chopped)
- Vegan cream cheese (1/2 cup)
- Black pepper (1/2 teaspoon)

Directions

1. Add water to rice cooker along with potatoes and cauliflower.
2. Cook for 30 minutes until potatoes and cauliflower are soft. Add green onions and stir.
3. Transfer to a bowl and add remaining ingredients. Mash until thoroughly combined.
4. Serve.

Nutritional Information

Calories 175.4

Carbs 24.7g

Protein 5.3g

Fat 7g

Curried Quinoa

Serves: 2

Preparation Time: 40 minutes

Ingredients

- Olive oil (2 tablespoons)
- Garlic (2 cloves, minced)
- Vegetable broth (2 cups)
- Ancho chile powder (1 tablespoon)
- Black pepper
- Onion (1, chopped)
- Quinoa (1 cup)
- Curry powder (1 tablespoon)
- Salt

Directions

1. Heat oil in rice cooker and sauté garlic and onion for 5 minutes.
2. Add remaining ingredients and stir to combine. Cook for 30 minutes or until thoroughly cooked.
3. Serve.

Nutritional Information

Calories 473

Carbs 62.8g

Protein 13.5g

Fat 19.8 g

Spicy Beans, Rice and Corn

Serves: 4

Preparation Time: 35 minutes

Ingredients

- Rice (1 cup)
- Sweetcorn (1 cup)
- Green pepper (1, chopped)
- Cumin (1 teaspoon)
- Black pepper
- Beans of choice (1 cup, cooked)
- Onion (1/2, chopped)
- Vegan bouillon (1 teaspoon, low salt)
- Chili powder (1 teaspoon)
- Water (2 cups)
- Lemon (1/2, juiced)
- Avocado (1)

Directions

1. Add rice to rice cooker then add corn and beans.
2. Add green pepper and onion followed by spices and bouillon and vegetables.
3. Add water and cook for 15-20 minutes or until thoroughly cooked.
4. Fluff rice and serve topped with mashed avocado and lemon juice.

Nutritional Information

Calories 687

Carbs 108g

Protein 19.7g

Fat 23.3 g

Chickpea, Red Lentil and Pumpkin Curry

Serves: 4

Preparation Time: 60 minutes

Ingredients

- Chickpeas (30 oz., drained)
- Garlic (2 cloves, diced)
- Red lentils (1 cup, rinsed)
- Curry powder (1 tablespoon)
- Kosher salt (1 teaspoon)
- Yellow onion (1, diced)
- Vegetable broth (2 cups, low salt)
- Pumpkin puree (1 cup)
- Cayenne pepper (1/4 teaspoon)
- Coconut milk (15 oz., full fat)

Directions

1. Add all ingredients to rice cooker except milk. Stir to combine and cook for 40 minutes.
2. Add coconut milk and stir to combine, cook for an additional 20 minutes or until thick.
3. Keep warm until ready to serve.

Nutritional Information

Calories 466

Carbs 86g

Protein 15g

Fat 3.8 g

Vegetarian Minestrone

Serves: 8

Preparation Time: 45 minutes

Ingredients

- Vegetable broth (6 cups)
- Kidney beans (15 oz. can, drained)
- Celery (2 ribs, chopped)
- Green beans (1 cup)
- Garlic (3 cloves, diced)
- Oregano (1 ½ teaspoons, dried)
- Thyme (3/4 teaspoon, dried)
- Macaroni (1/2 cup, elbow)
- Tomatoes (28 oz. can, crushed)
- Onion (1, chopped)
- Carrots (2, chopped)
- Zucchini (1, cubed)
- Parsley (1 tablespoon, fresh, diced)
- Salt (1 teaspoon)
- Black pepper (1/4 teaspoon)
- Spinach (4 cups, chopped)
- Vegan Parmesan cheese (1/4 cup, grated)

Directions

1. Add broth, kidney beans, celery, green beans, garlic, oregano, thyme, black pepper, tomatoes, onion, carrots, zucchini, parsley and salt to rice cooker.
2. Cook for 25 minutes then add macaroni and spinach; cook for an additional 15 minutes or until pasta is al dente.
3. Serve topped with cheese.

Nutritional Information

Calories 138

Carbs 25.2g

Protein 6.9g

Fat 1.7 g

Rice Cooker Applesauce

Serves: 4

Preparation Time: 20 minutes

Ingredients

- Apples (4, diced)
- Brown sugar (1/4 cup, vegan friendly)
- Cinnamon stick (1)
- Lemon juice

Directions

1. Combine all ingredients in a ceramic container that can fit in your rice cooker.
2. Put about 2 inches of water in your rice cooker and put in ceramic bowl.
3. Cook for 15 minutes and keep warm for 10 minutes.
4. Remove bowl from cooker, stir and adjust flavors if necessary.
5. Cool and serve.

Nutritional Information

Calories 143

Carbs 37.6g

Protein 0.5g

Fat 0.3 g

Coconut Tapioca Pudding

Serves: 6

Preparation Time: 1 hour 10 minutes

Ingredients

- Coconut milk (3 ¼ cups, unsweetened)
- Sugar (3/4 cup, vegan friendly)
- Salt
- Pearl tapioca (3/4 cup, small)
- Egg (1, beaten)
- Vanilla (2 ½ teaspoons)

Directions

1. Add all ingredients excluding vanilla to rice cooker and mix together.
2. Cook on 'porridge' mode or for 60 minutes. Be sure to check every 20 minutes and stir.
3. Add vanilla and stir. Cool, cover and refrigerate.
4. Serve.

Nutritional Information

Calories 422.9

Carbs 45.6g

Protein 3.6g

Fat 26.9 g

Rice Cooker Rice Pilaf

Serves: 6-8

Preparation Time: 25 minutes

Ingredients

- Jasmine Rice (1 ½ cups)
- Silvered almonds (1/4 cup)
- Onion (1/2, diced)
- Garlic (2 cloves, diced)
- Vegetable broth (2 cups)
- Mushrooms (1 cup, sliced)
- Butter (2 teaspoons, vegan)

Directions

1. Melt butter in a skillet and add garlic and onion to pot; sauté for 5 minutes until fragrant and slightly golden.
2. Add rice to cooker along with sautéed garlic and onion. Put in all remaining ingredients and stir.
3. Cook for 20 minutes and keep on warm for 10 minutes.
4. Fluff with a fork and serve!

Nutritional Information

Calories 227.6

Carbs 40.3g

Protein 6.2g

Fat 4.2 g

Rice Cooker Mexican Rice

Serves: 6

Preparation Time: 35 minutes

Ingredients

- Rice (1 cup, long grain)
- Tomato paste (3 oz.)
- Onion (1/2 cup, diced)
- Green chilies (2 oz., diced)
- Red pepper flakes
- Vegetable broth (2 ¼ cups, low salt)
- Garlic (1 clove, diced)
- Black pepper
- Parsley

Directions

1. Add all ingredients to rice cooker and stir to combine.
2. Cook for 25 minutes and then open rice cooker and let rice sit for 3 minutes.
3. Fluff with a fork and serve.

Nutritional Information

Calories 238.2

Carbs 40.9g

Protein 6.9g

Fat 7.5 g

Rice Cooker Fried Rice

Serves: 4

Preparation Time: 40 minutes

Ingredients

- Rice (2 cups)
- Peanut oil (1 tablespoon)
- Onion (1, sliced)
- Frozen vegetable mix (1 cup)
- Vegetable broth (2 cups)
- Garlic (1 teaspoon, diced)
- Soy sauce (2 tablespoons)
- Carrots (1/2 cup, shredded)

Directions

1. Heat rice cooker and add oil along with garlic and onion. Sauté for 5 minutes until tender.
2. Add rice to mixture and stir to combine. Put in broth and frozen vegetable mix.
3. Cook for 25 minutes. Open cooker and add soy sauce and carrots; cook for an additional 5 minutes.
4. Fluff and keep warm for 5 minutes.
5. Serve.

Nutritional Information

Calories 1258

Carbs 162g

Protein 26.3g

Fat 54.6 g

Lemon Rice

Serves: 3-4

Preparation Time: 45 minutes

Ingredients

- Rice (1 cup, long grain)
- Salt
- Lemon zest (2 teaspoons, freshly grated)
- Italian parsley (2 tablespoons, fresh)
- Vegetable broth (1 ½ cups)
- Garlic (1 clove)
- Butter (2 tablespoons, vegan)

Directions

1. Add rice to rice cooker then add broth and salt to taste; put garlic in the center of rice on top.
2. Cook rice for 20 minutes then add butter, parsley and zest. Stir to combine and cook for 10 more minutes.
3. Fluff rice using a fork and keep warm till ready to serve.
4. Discard garlic and serve.

Nutritional Information

Calories 339.5

Carbs 53.4g

Protein 5.7g

Fat 8.6 g

Caribbean Rice

Serves: 4

Preparation Time: 40 minutes

Ingredients

- Rice (1 cup, white)
- Parsley (1/4 cup)
- Garlic (1 clove, diced)
- Scallions (2, chopped)
- Coconut (1/3 cup, toasted)
- Red pepper (1/3 cup, diced)
- Coconut milk (1 cup, light)
- Jerk seasoning (1teaspoon)
- Thyme (1 sprig)
- Ginger (1 teaspoon, grated)
- Sweet potato (3/4 cup, minced)
- Raisins (1/3 cup)

Directions

1. Add all ingredients except raisins to rice cooker and stir to combine.
2. Cook for 30 minutes then add raisins and stir; cook for an additional 10 minutes.
3. Fluff with fork and serve.

Nutritional Information

Calories 292.4

Carbs 55.9g

Protein 6g

Fat 10.3 g

Rice Cooker Spanish Rice

Serves: 6-8

Preparation Time: 40 minutes

Ingredients

- Rice (2 cups, long grain)
- Tomato sauce (8 oz.)
- Salsa (1/4 cup)
- Chili powder (2 teaspoons)
- Onion (1, chopped)
- Water (1/2 cup)
- Green chilies (4 oz., diced)
- Water (1 cup)
- Stewed tomatoes (14 oz., Mexican style with liquid)
- Cumin (3/4 teaspoon)
- Garlic salt (3/4 teaspoon)
- Green pepper (1, diced)

Directions

1. Add all ingredients to rice cooker except ½ cup of water; stir to combine.
2. Cook rice for 30-40 minutes then check rice and add leftover water if necessary.
3. Fluff rice and serve.

Nutritional Information

Calories 255.3

Carbs 56.1g

Protein 5.7g

Fat 0.8 g

Rice and Black Beans

Serves: 4

Preparation Time: 35 minutes

Ingredients

- Rice (1 cup, uncooked)
- Vegetable broth (14 oz. can)
- Sweet corn (14 oz., can)
- Canned tomatoes (10 oz., drained and diced)
- Green chilies (1 teaspoon)
- Black beans (15 oz. can)

Directions

1. Add all ingredients to rice cooker and stir to combine.
2. Cook for 30 minutes.
3. Fluff with a fork and keep warm for 5 minutes.
4. Serve.

Nutritional Information

Calories 306.9

Carbs 60.2g

Protein 12.9g

Fat 1.2 g

Rice Cooker Vegan Pancake

Serves: 3

Preparation Time: 20 minutes

Ingredients

- Flour (1 ¼ cups)
- Baking powder (2 teaspoons)
- Water (1 ¼ cups)
- White sugar (2 tablespoons, vegan friendly)
- Salt (1/2 teaspoon)
- Oil (1 tablespoon)

Directions

1. Sift all dry ingredients into a bowl and make a well in the center. Combine water and oil and pour into center and combine mixture together.
2. Use cooking spray to coat rice cooker and add batter to cooker. You may also choose to cook the batter a little at a time if you prefer. Close cooker and cook for 10 minutes.
3. Keep on warm for 5 minutes and remove.
4. Slice and serve.

Nutritional Information

Calories 264

Carbs 48.9g

Protein 5.4g

Fat 5.1 g

Carrot Rice with Peanuts

Serves: 6

Preparation Time: 30 minutes

Ingredients

- Rice (1 cup, long grain)
- Roasted peanuts (1/4 cup)
- Onion (1, sliced)
- Carrot (3/4 cup, grated)
- Black pepper
- Water (2 cups)
- Vegan butter (1 tablespoon)
- Ginger (1 teaspoon, diced)
- Salt to taste

Directions

1. Melt butter in rice cooker and add onion, ginger and carrots to pot. Sauté until fragrant and onion gets soft.
2. Add rice, water, black pepper and salt to pot and mix together.
3. Cook for 25 minutes. While rice cooks, grind peanuts in a processor and add to rice after it has finished cooking.
4. Fluff rice and keep warm for 10 minutes before serving.

Nutritional Information

Calories 199

Carbs 30g

Protein 4.8g

Fat 6.9 g

Vegan White and Black Bean Soup

Serves: 6

Preparation Time: minutes

Ingredients

- Olive oil (1 tablespoons)
- Celery (1 rib, chopped)
- Thyme (1 teaspoon)
- Vegetable broth (6 cups)
- White beans (14 oz. can, drained)
- Onion (1, chopped)
- Garlic (3 cloves, crushed)
- Black beans (14 oz. can, drained)
- Cumin (1 teaspoon)
- Sage (1/2 teaspoon)

Directions

1. Heat oil in rice cooker and add garlic, onion, thyme and celery. Cook for 5 minutes then add all remaining ingredients and mix together.
2. Cook for 30 minutes until and keep warm until ready to serve.

Nutritional Information

Calories 222

Carbs 37.3g

Protein 11.1g

Fat 3.5g

Rice Cooker Vegan Frittata

Serves: 2

Preparation Time: 40 minutes

Ingredients

- Shiitake mushrooms (2, sliced thin)
- Leek (1/2, chopped)
- Silken tofu (6 oz.)
- Turmeric (1/4 teaspoon)
- Black salt (1/4 teaspoon)
- Baking powder (1/2 teaspoon)
- Olive oil
- Garlic (1 clove, diced)
- Kale (1/4 cup, cooked)
- Nutritional yeast (1 tablespoon)
- Nutmeg (1/8 teaspoon, ground)
- Chickpea flour (1/4 cup)
- Soy milk (1/4 cup)

Directions

1. Heat skillet and add a little olive oil then add in garlic, leeks and mushrooms; sauté for 3 minutes, adding salt to taste. Remove from heat and put aside.
2. Add tofu, turmeric, salt, baking powder, soy milk, yeast, nutmeg and flour to processor and pulse until smooth. Transfer batter to a bowl and add vegetables; mix together.
3. Use oil or cooking spray to coat rice cooker and add batter. Cook for 40 minutes and then turn off rice cooker.
4. Cool and take frittata from cooker.
5. Slice and serve.

Nutritional Information

Calories 528

Carbs 124g

Protein 21g

Fat 17 g

Pomegranate and Quinoa Salad

Serves: 4

Preparation Time: 30 minutes

Ingredients

- Quinoa (2 cups, rinsed)
- Salt to taste
- All spice (1/2 teaspoon, powder)
- Pine nuts (toasted)
- Olive oil
- Water (4 cups)
- Pomegranate seeds (1 cup)
- Mint (1/2 cup, fresh, chopped)
- Lemon juice
- Black pepper

Directions

1. Add water and quinoa to rice cooker; add salt to taste and stir.
2. Cook quinoa for 25 minutes and remove from rice cooker. Add lemon juice and all spice, mix together and put aside to cool.
3. Add remaining ingredients and gently toss.
4. Serve

Nutritional Information

Calories 403

Carbs 39g

Protein 8g

Fat 4g

Rice Cooker Cabbage Stir Fry

Serves: 4

Preparation Time: 40 minutes

Ingredients

- Vegetable oil (1 tablespoon)
- Cabbage (2 cups, shredded)
- Carrots (1 cup, shredded)
- Salt
- Pepper
- Bell peppers (1/2 cup, cut into strips)
- Onion (1/2 chopped)
- Garlic (1 clove, diced)

Directions

1. Heat oil in rice cooker and add garlic and onion. Sauté until garlic is fragrant them all remaining ingredients and stir.
2. Cook for 20 minutes or until desired doneness is achieved.
3. Serve.

Nutritional Information

Calories 96

Carbs 8.4g

Protein 1.5g

Fat 6.9 g

Rice Cooker Smoky Orange Rice

Serves: 6

Preparation Time: 30 minutes

Ingredients

- Basmati rice (2 cups, washed)
- Saffron (powdered)
- Salt
- Butter (2 tablespoons, vegan friendly)
- Water (2 cups)
- Onion (1, diced)
- Pepper
- Lemon zest (1 teaspoon)
- Orange zest (1 teaspoon)
- Chipotle (1 teaspoon, chopped)

Directions

1. Add all ingredients to rice cooker and cook for 25 minutes.
2. Fluff and keep warm for 5 minutes.
3. Serve.

Nutritional Information

Calories 269.8

Carbs 49.5g

Protein 5.1g

Fat 5.6 g

Rice Cooker Jamaican Grits

Serves: 2

Preparation Time: 35 minutes

Ingredients

- Hominy (16 oz.)
- Grits (1/2 cup)
- Salt (1 teaspoon)
- Pimientos (1 teaspoon, crushed)
- Water (2 cups)
- Garlic powder (1/4 teaspoon)
- Vegan Cheddar (1 cup, shredded)
- Coconut cream (1/4 cup)

Directions

1. Soak hominy overnight in water.
2. Add grits and coconut cream to soaked hominy and cook for 20 minutes.
3. Add spices to mixture and stir; add salt to taste.
4. Top with cheese and keep warm till cheese melts.
5. Serve.

Nutritional Information

Calories 502

Carbs 70g

Protein 17.8g

Fat 20 g

Thanks for stopping by my little world, & I hope you enjoyed at least some of the recipes. I know that we all cannot like every single one, so hope that there were some you enjoy.

If you leave a review, thanks in advance. I really appreciate that, and if you go through all of my titles, which is well over 100+ now, I really try and do my best to comment, and say thanks on the reviews. I generally get to most of them.

CARPE DIEM

DEXTER

Check out other Amazon best sellers from the Recipe Junkie family! Just click the images.

50 Rice Cooker Recipes

RICE RICE BABY

Dexter Poin

The 2nd Coming
Of Riced

2

The information provided in this book is designed to provide helpful information on the subjects discussed. This book is not meant to be used, nor should it be used, to diagnose or treat any medical condition. For diagnosis or treatment of any medical problem, consult your own physician. The publisher and author are not responsible for any specific health or allergy needs that may require medical supervision and are not liable for any damages or negative consequences from any treatment, action, application or preparation, to any person reading or following the information in this book. References are provided for informational purposes only and do not constitute endorsement of any websites or other sources. Readers should be aware that the websites listed in this book may change.

These recipes are not intended to be any type of Medical advice. ALL individuals must consult their Doctors first and should always receive their meal plans from a qualified practitioner. . These recipes are not intended to heal, or cure anyone from any kind of illness, or disease.

Printed in Great Britain
by Amazon

57495222R00036